Broken, Shattered & healed

restoration of a shattered spirit

Denise Gardner

Broken, Shattered & Healed
"Restoration of a Shattered Spirit"
By Denise Gardner

Cover Designed by Denise Gardner
Published by Jazzy Kitty Publications
Logo Designs by Andre M. Saunders/Jess Zimmerman
Editor: Anelda L. Attaway

© 2021 Denise Gardner
ISBN 978-1-954425-16-3
Library of Congress Control Number: 2021903759

DEDICATION

I dedicate this book in memory of my mother, Nora L. McPherson. You never gave up on me and believed in me even when I gave you no reason to believe. Thank you for your loyalty towards me and your undying love. Thank you for the strength you showed towards our family and the true character of a strong woman. Even in adversity, you stood strong and fought for what you thought was right even when the odds were against you. I love you and I miss you, although your presence is always with me.

I also dedicate this book to every woman going through or who has overcome adversity in their life. May you be encouraged that there is hope and there is life after the pain. Remain strong in your faith.

ACKNOWLEDGMENTS

I thank God for coming into my life as Lord and Savior. I thank Him for His grace and mercy that He has shown me throughout this journey. I give Him all the honor and the glory. Without Him, none of this would be possible.

I a special thank you to my sister, Patricia Henderson-Betton, for all your love and support and for standing by me through this journey. Thank you for the sacrifices that you made. I know it wasn't easy, but I thank you for it all.

Thank you to my beautiful daughter, DeAja, who inspires and pushes me every day with her words of encouragement. I love you and thank you for always having "mommy's" back. Thank you for your loving and forgiving spirit.

Thank you to my niece, Teryan, for sharing your mom over the years. I love you, and I know that it wasn't always easy to do. Thank you for your understanding and for loving your cousin like a sister.

A special thank you to my former Bishop and Pastor. Thank you, Bishop Matthew Haskell, Jr., for the word that you have poured into my life through your messages of encouragement. My life has forever changed. Thank you, Pastor Monica, for being the best pastor and coach. Thank you for empowering me and helping me believe that I could do this.

A special thank you to my mentor and sister in the faith, Brenda Bynum. From the first day that I met you, you have been encouraging me to be my best. You pushed me when I didn't want to go any further, and you prayed more for me than I prayed for myself. I cherish our relationship with the utmost respect.

Thank you to my current Pastor, Dr. Rosa Smith-Williams. You are an awesome pastor and mentor. Thank you for always encouraging me.

"I Love You All…"

TABLE OF CONTENTS

INTRODUCTION

"For I know the plans I have for you, says the Lord. They are plans for good and not for disaster, to give you a future and a hope." Jer. 29: 11

Broken, Shattered & Healed is an inspirational story inspired by the personal struggles after years of abuse, alcohol dependency, abandonment, and depression. It is a journey of downward and upward spirals I faced and overcoming the obstacles and the journey it took to get back on the right path to pursue my purpose in life. It is by no means a self-help book but rather a testimonial of how God took a broken and shattered vessel and mended the pieces together and broke the chains of the past.

This process ultimately led to my being set free from people and a torn past. This book is meant to inspire every woman who has a broken past to understand that life doesn't have to end because of what was. There is hope, and there is a future awaiting you. Nothing that you have done has to keep you where you are. There is healing, and God wants to restore you to your rightful place. You may have been broken, and your spirit may have been shattered. But God is waiting to restore all that was taken from you and move you into this life of hope and purpose. Be encouraged as you read these pages and find hope in knowing that there is life after the pain. Be restored in Jesus' Name, Amen.

CHAPTER 1
Insight/The Beginning

Life throws things at us so quickly until sometimes, it is impossible to dodge the hurts and fears that life sends our way. I have known for a while that God has a purpose for my life.

It is not by coincidence that I was hit by a car at the age of eight in Washington, D.C., flipped over the front end of the car, over the roof and down the back, and walked away. It is not a coincidence that I was cut, ran over, and beaten day and night for five years, taken from my mother's home in a car, and drug by my hair, and still, I am here to tell my story. No, it is not a coincidence, but it was all to fulfill my purpose in life. I didn't understand that back then, but I do now. I ran for years, trying to escape God and his plans for my life. It was during those years that I battled some storms. During those years, life beat up on me so severely that there were days I no longer wanted to live.

I know that God has a designed purpose just for me. When I started this journey, I did not know what purpose or what destiny even meant. Even though I did not know what purpose was, I knew that there was something that I was meant to do and that all this hell I was going through was for a reason. I just did not know what.

I am a domestic violence survivor. I know without a shadow of a doubt that it is only by the grace of God that I am still here. When I began this journey, I thought that my reason for surviving was to help other women who have been and who still are victims of domestic violence find a way out. As I continue down this pathway of life, I find that the call is so much more profound.

Not only am I a victim of domestic violence, but I am also a victim of years of pain and brokenness that stems way back to my childhood.

Whoever said that your past does not affect your future never felt real pain. Looking back over my past, it had a significant effect on the paths that I chose. Do not misunderstand what I am trying to say.

Your past does not have to define your future, but your past can significantly affect when you reach your destiny without a reason to keep going (purpose) and direction.

I have always liked writing. It's as though when I write, I get a chance to say all I want to say. I can express how I feel and speak my truth. When I first felt the urge to write my story, God planted the title in my spirit. I remember saying to Him that no one wanted to hear my drama. I doubted myself, and I began to doubt that God had given me this message. It's imperative to keep in tune with the Holy Spirit, or you will talk yourself out of doing what it is you're meant to do and miss an opportunity to be a part of what God is doing here on the earth. I remember reading Pastor Rick Warren's book "The Purpose Driven Church." In his book, Pastor Warren wrote that God takes individuals just like me that are torn and broken and uses their hurt and pain to minister to others. Wow! So, all those trials, all the pain, hurt, and disappointments were not to break me but make me stronger and build me up for this moment. For every disappointment, there was a lesson to be learned.

You are your biggest advocate. Do not wait for someone to speak over your life. Speak over yourself. Healing does not come as a quick fix. It is a process that happens over time. Setbacks come, but you must push your way through. So, I began to write things down, and as I started writing, I began to notice something. In my writing, I found that my spirit had been broken way before adulthood, and I began to see myself as damaged goods. I was damaged from childhood. That was a lot to say. I Had terrific parents whom I love dearly and miss every day. However, there were some issues there.

Issues that deeply affected my childhood. It was a hard thing to admit at first. I had to admit that what I knew to be a loving home was a dysfunctional home that seemed to work or that I wanted to believe worked. Although I had the love of my parents, there were times that I questioned their love as a child. I understand alcoholism now, and I can see that both my parents were indeed alcoholics, although I am sure neither would have agreed to that fact. Despite that fault, I know that my parents loved my sister and me, and I can say we were cared for with the best they had to offer.

In my early childhood memories, I can remember being shuffled back and forth among family members. I never knew why this happened, but it was the beginning of a trend to see most of my young childhood into young adulthood. This bothered me, but as a child, you did not get to question adults' actions. You did what you were told to do, and that was that. Even as an adult, I never asked the question of why I was shuffled back and forth. Sometimes I think I did not honestly want to know the answer. There were times that I felt rejected and abandoned. I wondered if they loved me, or was I a disappointment to them, so early on, I learned about abandonment even though I did not know what the word meant. I was very close to my father. Some would have called me a real daddy's girl, and I was proud of that. As I grew up, I watched my mom and how she and my father interacted. The one thing that I know is that they loved each other, and when my dad died, a piece of her died with him. After he passed, I never saw real happiness in her again. Now that I think about it, I don't think I felt genuine happiness either.

During those times in her life, I saw lots of pain, and my mother just seemed to exist day in and day out.

Alcohol became her comforter. I adopted some of my mother's coping strategies to deal with hurt and disappointment as I grew into a young woman.

I learned in life to use alcohol as a crutch to lean on. It became a way of numbing myself so that I could not feel. I also learned to love at any cost. I learned to make it work even if it cost me my happiness. I buried myself in my pain. The sad thing was that the majority of my pain came from family. You would think that your family would have your back at all costs. That may be true in some cases, but it wasn't in mine. I endured hearing the "You're just like your mother," "You won't be nothing," "Look at you, who wants you," and so much more. I heard this before I even reached my teenage years. I heard it all, and I took it all in. I buried it all deep inside, and I pretended that none of it mattered. That's why I couldn't understand after my father's death how my mother could leave me with family in one state while she handled business affairs in another. There came that feeling of abandonment again. I could not understand why she could not see that this was not best for me.

I felt that she did not care, and I developed resentment against her. It didn't help that my sister and I were separated, and that separation would last almost into both our young adult lives. I thought no one wanted me and that they just left me there to endure whatever may happen. I was outraged, and I felt further rejection. I learned to keep life moving, but on the inside and every time I looked in the mirror, those phrases would ring in my ears and what I saw in the mirror was nothing. Everything around me was dark, and I felt lost. I felt that there was nothing for me and that my life was destined to be nothing. As an adult, I know now that this was not the case and that my mother loved me beyond and back. She could not have known the pain and rejection that I felt as a child because I never told her what I felt when I wasn't with her. I never told her, not even before she died all that I went through and thought as a child.

I say to you, be careful of the words that you speak out of your mouth.

You have no idea the power of the words you speak. Not only that, be extremely watchful of who you let speak into your life. Be protective of yourself. Not everyone has your best interest at heart. Watch with whom you share your dreams. I have come to learn that the people you think are happy for you aren't. You have those fakers who pretend to care, but when times get hard, they back away.

Then you have those who are genuine.

There are some out there. Those who aren't afraid to check you when you're wrong, encourage you when you're down, and celebrate when you succeed. Remember always to cherish those few because they don't come along often. I wish I had known that back then. Oh, the grief I could have spared myself. Until this day, I remember the words that changed my life forever. No matter how I tried to shake the words from my head, they haunted me and taunted me into adulthood. The pain was worse because I admired the person who spoke the words to the point that I wanted to be just like them. The words that were said to me penetrated deep.

To hear someone that I loved thought of me as a disappointment, and I would never be anything hurt. It changed me. It made me see what I saw as life differently. As time went on, I started to put up wall after wall after wall. I learned not to trust people, and I learned not to believe in myself. I eventually learned not only to expect people to put me down, but I learned to put myself down, and I was good at it. I felt extremely unworthy of anything. I looked for nothing. I gave nothing, and I asked for nothing in return. My self-esteem hit rock bottom, and I couldn't find a place to fit in. I didn't fit in with family, and I didn't fit in with the people I hung around. I couldn't find common ground with anyone.

This was a confusing time in my life. I couldn't grasp things; nothing about my life made sense to me. I couldn't understand why my father died when I was eight and left me alone. I couldn't understand why my mother moved our family to North Carolina after his death.

I couldn't understand why I experienced childhood trauma into young adulthood. I couldn't understand why I thought all of this was normal. I couldn't grasp any of this. Back then, I knew who God was. I didn't have a relationship with Him, but I did believe He existed. I heard others talk about the goodness of God and how they were blessed, but I didn't have that for myself, nor did I think that I could or would have a blessed life. I didn't even know what a blessed life was. I had more questions than I had answers. I learned to repress things, and up went more walls. I became my safe haven, and I lived behind a mask. I made up in my mind that no one would ever hurt me again and that I was my only protector. I held every hurt, anger, and disappointment inside of me, and I trained myself not to feel anything. No one should have that type of power over your life. I understand now that no one has that much power over you unless you give it to them. You are the captain of your ship. Stop letting others take the rudder of your life.

I overcame some things, or so I thought. There were times that I fought hard to win the love and acceptance of the people that I loved, even though these were the people that hurt me the most. I still wanted and needed their approval and love.

Let me change that. I thought that these were the people that I needed. I did all the right things and tried to be the person I thought would make them happy. That was my biggest mistake. I tried to lead a life that would make other people happy. You can't live your life through someone else's eyes.

What people want from you is what's going to benefit them. It has nothing to do with you and everything to do with what they can get from you. The majority of the things I did to please others benefited me in no way at all, but I did what I thought I needed to do. I tortured myself, and I reached my lowest, trying to be a people pleaser.

When it didn't work, I tried harder until I had nothing else to offer. I was so used to other people making decisions for me; it was hard for me to learn to handle things independently. I became dependent on other people, and they used it to their advantage. Dependency on others is dangerous. I'm finding that not only is it dangerous, but it's also unhealthy. I remember the words my Aunt spoke to her son and me before she died. She told us to be careful of who we entrusted to make decisions for you because they would begin to make decisions without you sooner or later.

That was a powerful statement, but how true it was. The worst feeling ever is not to have a say in your own life. I started to become defensive, and I put on the mask of being a tough girl. I tried to convince myself and others around me that I could handle anything, and nothing bothered me. I wore the mask well, I thought, but inside, the pain and anger laid dormant for years. I wasn't okay, and everything was not fine. Life would soon prove that there was much in store for me.

Not everything about my life has been wrong. I managed to get back on track but only for a moment. When life got too complicated and things didn't go as I wanted them to go, I would fall back into my old pattern of self-destructive behavior. I became my own worst enemy. I didn't think many things through, and I made some bad choices that eventually would come back to haunt me. However, when it was good, it was good, and that's the way life is. You have your highs and your lows. It's what you do during these times that makes the difference.

Life came at me so fast, and I was so unprepared for what it had to offer. It was as if I were a drifter moving from one place to the next, not belonging anywhere. I had no direction in life and no idea how to find one. I was scared. I was angry, and I was lost. I didn't trust anyone, not even myself. I didn't have anyone to confide my pain to. Remember when I said to cherish and not take advantage of those relationships with those who have your best interest at heart? Too bad I didn't have the common sense to take my advice. I burnt a few bridges and lost some people along the way that cared about me. Some were repaired, and some lost forever. Sure, I had my mom, but her life wasn't faring well for her, either. I saw no need to lay more burdens on her even though as I look back on it now, that's precisely what I did. My mom never gave up on me. The real truth, she was the only one who ever really believed in me, and I was so ungrateful. I see that now. I was bitter, and I took it out on everyone, including my mom. I gave my mother so much grief. Even so, that woman loved me with all she had in her heart to give up until the day she died. She did whatever she had to do to make me feel loved. The day she died was another hard blow to me. Someone else that I loved and who loved me was taken away.

Let me put this in right here.

You never know what tomorrow holds. When I say that I was lost, I was lost. Have you ever been in a room filled with people, but you felt as though you were the only one there? Yeah, that was me, all alone. The loneliest place to be is with yourself, especially when you're in a dark place.

I don't know how many pity parties I threw for myself. It was always someone else's fault that things were terrible in my life. I felt like everyone was against me and that no one cared whether I lived or died. I cried on anyone's shoulder that would listen. Somehow every conversation ended up about how someone did me wrong and that they would one day get what was coming to them for the wrong they had done to me. I was good at feeling bad for myself, and I wanted everyone else to feel as bad as I did.

Again, I say I was my own worst enemy.

I know now that you can't focus on all the wrong and the what-ifs. We all sometimes feel in our lives that we were dealt a bad hand in life. You can't dwell on those things. The more you dwell on the darkness, the darker it gets.

I held so many pity parties until I got tired of being the guest of honor. I had friends that I hung out with at times. Even though they eventually got tired of hearing the poor me stories until, one by one, some of those friendships faded into the dark. Be wary of people who join in and encourage this kind of behavior. As I said before, everyone has an agenda, but the agenda isn't clear.

You have to be able to determine who is really on your team. You have to be able to discern why they are on the team. Are they trying to pull you out or waiting for your downfall? Still, others are just enablers unable to help themselves; nonetheless, help you. I went to school and worked just like everyone else; however, I was only going through living motions. You know, get up each morning not knowing what to expect from the day. I just wanted to get through each day. But every day was the same, and every day was like there was no end. I felt dead inside. I didn't feel anything. I didn't know how to feel, and I didn't know what to feel. I just existed. I don't want to come off and pretend that all of my life was a disaster. Again, life had its highs and lows. When it was good, it was good. What I am saying is that if you are not careful, the hurts of the past can and will catch up with you, and if you don't deal with the hurts, it can alter when and if you will ever fulfill the purpose in life and the destiny that God has prepared just for you. Even in that state of mind, I felt that there had to be more. This could not be all that life was meant to be.

The problem was, I didn't know how to find that more. I wanted more. I needed more, but I didn't know what to do to get to the more. If you're like me, you have asked yourself, "Why am I here?" I went through a lot in life, and truth be told, in the natural eye, I shouldn't be here, but I am. It's a good question. We go about our everyday lives going back and forth, not knowing that we are here on this earth because our Heavenly Father has a purpose for our life that only as an individual you can fulfill. A purpose that he designed especially for you. The problem is that we get caught up in life that we just go on living without direction. When it comes down to it, you're not living but existing.

Until you figure out why you are here, you will always just exist. When you reach that point in your life, you need to dig deeper. That's when you know it's not the time to give up. It was during those times that I wished that I had known how to pray. I mean, really pray. Instead of reaching out to others and looking to God, I withdrew further into my shell. Up went more walls and the darker that place became for me. It was during those darker times that I would learn life's biggest lessons. Never give up. Push harder.

It was during those dark times that I learned to push through the pain. Although I was broken, I had to believe that I would make it out, and my life would be restored. There was a reason for my being here, and there is a purpose that God has designed specifically with me in mind that only I can fulfill. So, no matter what I've been through, I understood that I had to push and keep going. I wasted so much time while destiny and purpose were waiting for me. It was my time to press towards my destiny and the life that God created for me.

CHAPTER 2

Downward Spiral

It doesn't matter how many times you say that you're moving forward with your life if all you're doing is saying the words but showing no real commitment going forward. I thought that I was on the right track. Life was going well for me. I had overcome some obstacles and accomplished some of the goals that I had set for myself. The job was going well. Living on my own and being self-sufficient was awesome and fulfilling. I was growing spiritually, and my relationship with my family was progressing. Yes, I would say life was going well. What more could I ask? The biggest mistake you can make is to think that nothing can go wrong when life is going well for you. You get so caught up in the good that you forget how you got there. It takes hard work and determination, and many prayers to move from the dark to the light. During the time I was trying to achieve some things, I stayed on my knees. I sought help and asked questions on how to obtain what I needed to make life work for me. I was exercising my faith, and I believed that what I wanted to achieve, I could. It's what happened after I had cleared some hurdles that led to my downfall. This all goes back to what I said earlier about being the captain of your ship and taking charge of your own life. You can't let everybody and everything enter into your mind. Don't second guess what you have set out to do in life by listening to what others have to say about your dreams. They're your dreams, and everybody is not on board to see you fulfill them, nor do you want them to be.

For so long, I dwelled on how people perceived me. I cared about what they thought, and their opinions mattered. Most of my life was spent trying to be what others thought I should be. When it came time for me to step up and be who I wanted to be, it was hard. I didn't trust my judgment, and I second-guessed every idea that came to me and every decision I had to make. I put people in my business. I put people in my business that didn't have any business of their own or either they couldn't handle their own lives. I literally could not think for myself. The more I listened to people, the more I lost who I was and adapted to their way of thinking.

The one thing I learned throughout this process is the power of persuasion. Very little of what was being said to me was ever on the positive side.

There were always those comments of "you're not going to make it," "that's not for you," and so much more.

Pretty soon, I had convinced myself that maybe they were right, and I was biting off more than I could chew. I'm sure we have all had this happen. Here is where you have to choose to push past the negativity and become who you were meant to be. Unfortunately, I learned all this after making some dreadful mistakes that cost me dearly. I was at the top of my game, and once again, I lost my focus. Even though I had physically moved on to start this new life, I was mentally stuck in the same place. Every opportunity I got, I revisited my past, and that came back to haunt me later.

I had this new life, but I wasn't moving with it. I was still stuck in the past. My life consisted of home, work, and the church in that order. I didn't branch out past that zone. I knew people from work and church, and my sister had introduced me to her friends, but those were just cordial relationships and nothing outside of that. Needless to say, it got boring fast, and I became lonely, and my loneliness led me to make some bad decisions. I had disassociated myself with people I sought after their friendships, knowing this would not be healthy for me, but I pursued them anyway. Remember this; your past is just that, your past. Don't get stuck on the way things used to be.

You have got to learn to leave all that drama behind you, or you'll never be able to move forward with your life.

It doesn't mean that you don't care about the people you left behind, and it doesn't mean that you think you're better than them. Don't let people lay that guilt trip on you with the *"don't forget where you come from"* line. You will never forget, but don't let it dictate the rest of your life. Learning to move forward shows that you have decided to move past what was holding you from your destiny, and now you are pressing your way into the life that you are meant to live and become the person you were designed to be. This wasn't easy for me to do. I struggled day and night. These were people I had known most of my life, and this was the only life I knew.

Moving away from the known to the unknown was horrific, and I went into panic mode. I made excuses for myself of why this wasn't the right time for this kind of move. I tried to think of every reason, but none of them could I justify. So, I started entertaining my past. The more I entertained it; I slowly drifted back to the old lifestyle where I felt comfortable. As I said before, you will never truly forget where you came from or what you have been through. Sometimes you aren't ready or prepared to revisit where you once were. Some things have too much of a stronghold on you, and if you're not ready and equipped with the right tools, you can be drawn right back into the place that you escaped. I know this all too well. I had convinced myself that I had made a life for myself and my daughter in Delaware the same way I could do the same in North Carolina. Besides that, I told myself that's where my family and friends were, and that's where I belonged. I convinced myself that all it took was will-power and that I could make it. It wasn't long before I was right back in the place; I had fought so hard to get out of and doing the same old messy things all over again. When I made that first decision to move back to North Carolina, I kept my decision from my sister until I got ready for the final move. She didn't argue with me, nor did she try to change my mind. She told me one thing only and that my life was mine to do what I wanted but that she would not let me drag my daughter back into that life again. After a few "discussions," if that's what you would call it, I agreed. It wasn't like I had a choice. That was the one sensible decision I made. I want to say this: When making life-altering decisions, you have to step back and look at the whole picture, especially if there are children involved. You can't just think about yourself. I had done that too often and put my needs before my child's. I was very selfish, and it almost cost me losing my child. We all want to be happy, but at what cost? Is what you're seeking worth losing what you already have?

Don't base your happiness solely on emotions. Emotions can lead you down some dangerous paths. Unfortunately, at the time, I was thinking about my selfish agenda. I wasn't happy where I was, and I felt I deserved to live my life the way I wanted and make my own happiness. In the back of my mind, I wasn't thoroughly convinced about what I was doing.

Nothing worked out the way that I planned. I did get the job that I promised myself that I would get, but that was also soon gone. I found myself right back where I started from, depending on someone else to survive, and those old wounds were reopened, and all those broken emotions emerged back to the surface and landed me back into my private hell.

In the beginning, I had people trying to convince me to get out and go back to the life I left. Of course, I didn't want to hear any of that. In my mind, they didn't know the life I was living while I was gone and the loneliness that I had felt. I told them to mind their own business and that this was my life, and I would live it the way I wanted to. I was in control, but I wasn't. Sound familiar? How many times had I told myself that before? Nobody wants to be told that they're making a mistake, and no one wants to admit when they realize that they made that mistake after being forewarned. So, what did I do? I made a choice to be offended. Yes, I made a choice to be offended. Being Offensive is a choice, so I became defensive, and once again, I started the blame game all over again. I wasn't at the place that I could own up to my mistakes. You can't fix what you don't own up to. It's worth repeating. The fact is, you will repeat the same mistakes over and over until you learn that there is a lesson in the mistake. Until you learn the lesson, you'll relive the past over and over again.

This part of the journey would turn out to be my worst. I heard my pastor say that you allow your past to continue to come in unless you close the back door. That's exactly what I did. I kept flirting with what I had left behind. I entertained all the drama, and I invited it all back in. Once again, I lived in the drama-filled life that had caused me so much pain and had cost me everything that I had worked so hard to obtain. Why?

Because I didn't take the time to think and understand that what I had moved onto in life was the direction that I should follow, I let my fear of the unknown draw me back into a life of what I knew and what I felt comfortable with even though it meant me no good. Have you ever felt as though you were traveling in a circle, traveling the same path? Even worse, have you ever felt as though you were pushed into a hole, and the harder you tried to climb out of that hole, it seemed as though more dirt was being thrown on top of you? Well, that's what I was experiencing. I had dug this hole for myself so deep, and when I realized what I had allowed myself to do, I could not find an escape, a way out. I was trapped without a plan of escape. This time I could blame only myself for allowing the enemy once more the opportunity to come in and take control of my life. I became outraged. I was angry with everyone. I was mad at myself, but most of all, I was angry with God. Where was He when I needed Him, and how could He allow this to happen to me again? How could I be angry with God? I was that angry. I convinced myself that because I chose a life different than what he set for me, he turned his back and was punishing me. I knew better, but who better to blame. Where was he when I needed him, and why wasn't he coming to see about me?

The Holy Spirit indeed gives you a warning before destruction. The signs were there. I saw them but what I didn't do was heed the warnings. I was in a bad place. This time I was alone. I was once again cut off from my family in Delaware, and the family I had in North Carolina made it clear that they weren't going to get involved in my mess. I had burnt some much-needed bridges one too many times. I had to ask myself what choices I have now. I was at a fork in the road, and when I needed to reach out to some people, especially my sister, I couldn't. The one person I thought that I could count on outside my mother had now closed the door in my face. I couldn't understand how she could do that. I understand now, but then I was feeling some type of way towards her. I had the nerve to have an attitude with her for cutting me off. She quit answering my phone calls, text messages, and my letters.

Yeah, I was highly upset. I know now that she was doing what she had to do to keep herself together. For so long, she had carried me and my mess until it affected her and affected the whole family. She had to cut me off not only for my good but for hers also. I couldn't see that then when I tell you that the enemy has a plan for your life to bring you down and use anything and anybody, including yourself, believe it! I let the enemy use me to blame the one who always came to my rescue for my downfall. You don't know how many times since then that I have had to go back and apologize for what I put her and my family through. I was ungrateful, and I can admit that now. I was the one who lit the flame on something dead when the fire had gone out. I was entertaining dead situations, but instead of leaving the dead buried, I dug it up.

The situation in your life that you wanted to end so badly. Those relationships, whether personal or business. Whatever your case, God resolved it and closed the door. Instead of opening the door to that dead situation, leave the door closed and move past it. Now I was a prisoner trapped in a hole that I had dug. No matter which way I turned, I couldn't find a way out this time. I still had some team players who tried to be there for me, and they wanted to help me out the best they could even though their hands were tied, mainly by me. For a while, I was brainwashed into thinking that this was the best my life was ever going to be. That was the reason these things kept happening to me. I was led to believe that the people that I thought cared about me didn't.

I tried hanging on to my belief that life would change for me and that I would get out. At that point in my life, all I had was hope. That's what I held onto, hope.

Then there came that moment when I started to lose hope. I had prayed, pleaded, begged for this situation to turn around. I didn't want to admit that I had messed up, but the fact was I had to admit it. I finally had to own up to my mess. During that time, the few people that were cheering for me soon gave up on me. Here I was again. When I say I was on a downward spiral, that's an understatement. I was headed straight into a bottomless pit, and the elevator was descending swiftly.

There was a point that my life was twirling and swirling as if I were in a storm, which I was. I felt that I was drawn right into the eye of this storm, and I was being tossed to and forth from one side of the storm to the next. I was really being beaten up. This went on for months. I had no fight left in me. I had lost myself, and I didn't recognize myself. I had given up. I had given up on myself, life, and, most of all, I gave up on God. I stopped praying, and I didn't want to be around the people of God. I had lost my faith, and I had no hope. I went into therapy, thinking that if I talked to someone professionally, they could help me figure out how to turn this around. I went to A.A., hoping they could give me the answers. I went to other people searching for answers. I went to every source I knew, except for the one source that had all the answers, "God!" Nothing worked. I was looking for answers in all the wrong places.

I walked out of therapy just as broken as I went in. I walked right back into my living hell. I feel compelled to say this. There is nothing you have done so wrong that should cause you to give up on life. That is a trick of the enemy and a lie straight from the pit of hell. No matter what you have been through. No matter what they say about you, you matter, and your life does matter. You are somebody uniquely made with God's purpose in mind. I wish that I had heard those words, and I probably did but couldn't receive nor believe them at that time. You Matter!! Don't give up on yourself. I remember when my daughter was younger. She would come to me and say, "Mommy, we fall down, but we get up."

From the mouth of babes, we fall down, but when you fall, the key is not to stay down. Somehow, if you push yourself to your knees, you will find the strength to stand. My world was so out of control back then that if I had heard this, I don't know; maybe I would have fought a little harder. Don't get me wrong, I was at my breaking point, and I did try to fight. I knew if I ever quit entirely and lost all my fight, my life would be over. I had many dark days ahead of me, but I kept living, and I gave it all I had. I wanted to give up so many times. Whenever I got ready to throw in the towel, all I could hear was my little girl's voice saying to me, "We fall down, but we get up." When life gets you to that point, find a focal point. Find that one thing that matters and hold onto it and focus on it. Find your fight. This was all I had to hold onto. It kept me alive. Although my battle had just begun, I now had a new reason to fight and to hang in there.

It was hard, but in the end, I learned a more significant lesson. I was never in the fight alone.

CHAPTER 3

Downward/Upward Spiral

The dictionary defines the word spiraling as circling around a center at a continuously increasing or decreasing distance, to rise or fall with steady acceleration. That's how I would describe my life. I was spinning around at a rapid pace with no direction and no specific path. I had my high moments, and I had my low moments.

My life had been spiraling out of control for years, and life the way I had known it no longer existed. I started living a life that was full of blame. Who did I blame? Everybody, but mostly myself. No one wants to see themselves as the cause of their destruction. I got tired of blaming myself, and I convinced myself it had to be other people who caused me to go through so much pain. I took the focus off of me and placed that burden on those around me. I became what I thought people wanted me to be. For this to happen, I had to first put on my mask because what was behind the mask was weak and frail.

I had to become hard to the core.

Others were not my problem, and the only person I was concerned with was me. I didn't care whose feelings I hurt. Nobody ever cared about me and how I felt, so why should I care whose feet I stepped on. I was my only concern. I was a mess and headed down a dangerous road. The sad thing about it was that I was going along for the ride willingly.

As I have said before, I never had any real expectations out of life.

All my expectations and dreams had been stripped from me without me even knowing it. It keeps going back to what I said about giving people too much say over your life. At the end of the day, it all comes down to you. I came to that conclusion a day late and a dollar short. I had listened to so much negative spoken into my life that although I looked at it as a disguise, in actuality, this was the person that I had become. It wasn't long before the streets consumed me. There were times that I didn't know if I was coming or if I was going. In those upward spirals, I accomplished some things. I was able to go back to college and graduate with honors. I got married to who I now know was my best friend. Together, we could purchase a home, car, and we were blessed with a beautiful daughter. Let me say it was a process, and during that time, some major changes came first. In life, we are looking for a quick fix, and life doesn't happen like that.

You may get the quick fix, but it won't last. I had to experience that for myself. It was during this time that I had my first real encounter with God.

I say my first real encounter because, at first, I knew who God was, but during this upward spiral, I got to know Him personally. I had been in church most of my life, even sung in the choir, but that's all I did was attend church and served as church secretary. I had seen God move on other people's behalf, but I never dreamed or expected Him to do the same in my life. Who was I to think that I could ever be blessed or be a blessing? That was how my mind was programmed to think until I went to a meeting one night, and as the songwriter said, my heart wasn't right, but something got a hold of me. When I say it happened for me, it was as though the preacher had known me all my life and that he was preaching to me alone.

I couldn't wait to get to that altar.

Not only did I receive Christ, my husband and my best friend received Christ the same night. It seems as though that's how God works. I was positioned at the right place at the right time, and my family was saved. Don't shut God out. I know that it seems that He's so far away, when all along, He's right there waiting to be asked to come in. Did everything change right then? In some areas, yes. In other areas, it took some time, but a change did come. You have to remember all those habits were built up over the years, so a process had to be gone through, but it happened, and God blessed me. Needless did I know that while I was trying to live a Godly life, the enemy was setting a trap for me at the same time. I was doing everything I thought right. I was attending church, bible groups, serving in the church, praying, but I wasn't watchful, and the enemy snuck right in. Please remember this, in everything you do; the enemy doesn't want to see you happy. He will do what he has to do to make sure happiness is the last thing you will experience. The bible says that he is going back and forth throughout the earth, looking for whoever he can devour, and he doesn't care who he uses to bring about your destruction. Don't be complacent with where you are in your walk with Christ. You must stay vigilant before the Lord, praying over yourself and the ones you love. I slipped right there. I took my eyes off the cross, and it wasn't long before my life started into another downward spiral. As I said, the enemy doesn't care who he uses to bring you down. His only mission and concern are that you fall. Sometimes the person/persons being used don't know that they're being used. That's where your discernment comes in. I saw the signs and ignored them all. Suddenly, the church was not my number one priority. I found reasons not to go to church. I found ways to stay away from the saints even when they came to my house.

When I did go to church, the fire wasn't burning in my heart like it was before. I felt as though I was going out of an obligation. Before long, I quit going altogether. You can't entertain the enemy. The more I entertained the enemy, the further away from God I became. It wasn't long before things started falling apart. Of course, it started in my home. We were at each other's throats constantly, and every little detail became an issue. It wasn't long before I was back at my old game, the blame game once again. I blamed it all on my husband. He was the cause of the problems. He was the reason that bills weren't being paid. According to my report, I was doing what I was supposed to do, and as head of the household, all this was his responsibility, not mine. Now, I was the pawn working against myself. I let the enemy use me for my own downfall once again. It wasn't long before I was back in the streets doing what I knew best.

I turned back to my old friend, "alcohol." I didn't know much about alcoholism, but I understand it now. I grew up around drinkers, so I knew the effects that alcohol had on people. I knew how it affected me, but I knew I could depend on it to numb the pain when things went wrong. Slowly, I was forming an addiction to the thing that gave me comfort. I not only wanted it; I became dependent on it.

What is addiction? The dictionary defines addiction as a complex need that affects the functioning of both the brain and the body. As I researched the topic of alcoholism and addiction, I found that even though people were abusing alcohol, they were still able to function daily, working and leading what others saw as a normal life. That wasn't me. At first, I was able to go to work, manage my household, but as time went on, that wasn't my story. The more I drank, work became irrelevant. There were warning signs that this was turning into a problem. Some of the addiction symptoms are a severe loss of control, preoccupation with the drug, and failed attempts to quit. I can say I experienced all these symptoms. The more I drank, the more my demeanor changed.

There were times I didn't like myself and wanted to get away from myself. When I wasn't able to drink, I thought about drinking. I was like a child waiting to get to the toy store. I couldn't wait to get where it was. There were times that I wanted to quit. I didn't like what it was doing to my family or me, but it had me hooked. I became less and less like myself. I didn't recognize this person I was becoming, but I kept drinking even though it would cost me everything. That's the thing about addiction; after you do it for so long, it becomes normal, and you wonder why people are so uptight. At first, it was fun. I was just having fun, relieving some of the stress in my life. It became so much more.

It took over my life. Eventually, I lost my job. There were times that the money that was meant to pay bills, I used to drink. When I drank, everybody drank. Misery indeed loves company. I would buy drinks for people I knew didn't like me to have someone to drink with. I was spiraling out of control, and it got worse. We eventually lost the car and the home. You would think that would be a wake-up call. Well, it wasn't. Instead of trying to get help, I did the opposite. I went all in. My life was a mess already. What else could go wrong? I would soon find out that things could and would get worse. Until you walk in someone else's shoes, don't pass judgment.

I had done that on several occasions.

I would judge people's choices and swore that it would never be me, but it was me. I was in that same predicament, and now I was the one being judged.

You see, when things are going well for you, you have all the friends in the world. Again, I repeat, watch the people you surround yourself with. It was all good when I had something to offer them, but when the money was gone, so were they. They talked bad about me.

These were the same people that I called friends. My friends were now feeding me to the dogs. Some of the things that were being said were true, but oh, the lies they told.

Remember, the enemy doesn't care who he uses as long as it brings about his desired result, your downfall. My downfall did come and when it did, only a few friends stuck by my side. What I didn't know at the time but found out later, the ones that stayed with me were just as guilty as the ones that left. They were just smart enough to do their dirt secretly and stuck around to see the results. I'm not saying that everyone has your failure as their plan, which was also so in my case. I did have a few who did have my best interest, and those relationships still stand strong today

I'm so glad for my family. When I was at my worst, my sister was right there. She stepped in when no one else would. So much had been said to her, but instead of her using it against me, she didn't hesitate to take on the responsibility of taking my child and me into her home so that I could get my life back on track. I thank God for her every day. The trap the enemy set for me didn't bring about the results that he had hoped. I wasn't the best big sister, and I surely wouldn't have won any awards.

Alcohol had put an immense strain on our relationship.

When she could have had the opportunity to turn her back on me, she chose not to. That intervention saved my life and was a brand-new beginning for me, and I promised myself that I would make the best of the new opportunity. I was lucky; not everyone would have been so forgiving. Be careful not to burn bridges. Nurture those relationships that are important to you. You never know when you're going to need someone on your side. Second chances are hard to come by. Don't take them for granted. I used to think this is the hand life dealt me, and I lived with that fact. My perspective has now changed. Life may have dealt you a hand, but you determine what becomes of that hand by your choices. In the beginning, I was excited about having a fresh start in life. This was my second chance at a new life. I got a job and moved into my own apartment in less than a year. It wasn't easy, and I doubted that I could ever do it. There were several times that I wanted to throw in the towel. Life is scary, and failing was always upfront in my mind.

Don't let yourself talk you out of going for your dreams. I remember my sister sitting me down on the sofa one day and shared some things on her mind. In our conversation, she told me that she felt I had given up on life and that I was afraid to succeed because I felt unworthy of happiness. That was a statement I didn't expect. Did I take it for what it was worth? No, I automatically became defensive and offended. Remember, being offensive is a choice. At this time, I was choosing to be offended. Up went the walls again. You see, I hadn't learned to take constructive criticism at that point. Stop being so defensive. Sometimes God puts people in our paths to help in guiding us through the pathway of life. We don't always get to choose who that person will be. However, I felt about her comment; in the end, she was right. She hit the nail right on the head. I was scared to succeed. I don't know why. It just felt as though success was not an option for me. I kept fighting, although there were times that it seemed the more ground I would gain, there was always something that was holding me back. I later realized that the only thing that was holding me from reaching my goals was me. Despite how I felt, I kept pressing forward, not knowing where I was headed or what was in store for me. I remember the day my life took a turn for the better. My family visited a church one Sunday morning. The pastor told the story of young David and how all he had was his slingshot and his five smooth stones when he went up against Goliath. David didn't back down, and he didn't run away. He used what he had to bring the giant down. That message was so powerful, and I hung on to his every word. As I listened to this message, I felt hope rise in me again. I joined that church and became an active member of Prevailing Church International in New Castle, Delaware, Bishop Matthew Haskell, Jr., Founder. As I said, I felt hopeful again. I learned all that I know now about faith and how to pursue destiny and chasing after purpose, sitting under the teachings of this man of God. I was in a good place. I was finally living the life that I had longed to live. In my mind, nothing was going to stand in my way of happiness ever again, or so I thought. Why do we keep repeating the same mistakes over and over again? This was a question that I had to ask myself and one that I really wanted to know the answer to. I read a few articles on this subject and found it interesting that others also wanted to know the answer. One article that I read suggested that people who continuously repeat mistakes often do so right before a significant accomplishment or right after something good has happened. Where have I heard this before? Sounds a lot like self-sabotage to me. I've been there and done that many times. This usually happens due to overwhelming and anxiousness overtakes the person, and they end up pulling the rug right from under themselves.

I have done that too. It's kind of like protecting yourself from rejection or future rejections. The truth of the matter is it's a familiar pain you're causing with a sense of control. We hope to master the pain and come up with a new ending for the same story. What ends up happening is we don't master the pain or change the past and end up repeating the same things over and over. A sad story will always have a sad ending, no matter what happens. We keep involving ourselves with the same people and the same situations that caused us the pain to try to change the outcome and repeat the pattern repeatedly. I wanted to know if this caused me to keep making these same mistakes and how could I stop? There's only one way, identify the cause and understand why you make your choices. Every mistake has a lesson, and until you learn what the lesson is, you'll keep repeating the process. Take a reflective moment, and when you find yourself making the same mistakes, examine your attitude to see why you're not learning from the past and then come up with changes that will prevent you from making the same mistakes. It starts with you.

CHAPTER 4
The Turnaround

I wish I could say that the turning point in my life came suddenly, but it didn't. Things got worse before they got better. I was determined that this would be my last spiral and that I was planting myself on solid ground. I had to go through Hell before I got to this point. I sank into a deep depression. I didn't think well of myself and what I had become. I was broken. I was broken and shattered. I was living in a shell. Therapy didn't work for me. What good was therapy when I went back out into the same distort world built around me after leaving therapy? I got to the point where I decided that I didn't want to live. My family had already closed the door on me, so I decided that they wouldn't miss me and life would be better without me. You see, this is what the enemy aims to do. He knows that if he can get into your mind and attack you there, the rest will be easy. You have to protect what you listen to and what you choose to believe. I didn't want to live, but I was too scared to end my life also. I knew the word, and I knew what choosing to end my life would mean for my eternity. I may not have been living the principles, but I knew them. I started drinking even more. Remember, this was the only comfort that I knew that worked. The more I drank, the less I felt. Needless to say, I was killing myself very slowly.

I think that my turning point was having someone look at me one day and said to me, "Neicy, you know what people are saying about you? They're saying that you don't have anything going for yourself."

After saying what they said, they looked at me as though they expected me to respond. My response was, I walked away. I know that's not what they expected me to do, but that was all I had at that moment. What was I to say when they were right. When I was alone later that night, of course, I thought about what was said and reality set in. It was all true. I really didn't have anything going for myself, at least; that's what the enemy wanted me to believe.

There came that moment when I realized that what I had been doing was not living but existing. I had truly forgotten what life was all about. It all came back to putting on that mask and pretending that I was okay. This time I couldn't just put on the mask. Putting on the mask was not an option for me this time. I was tired of pretending that I was alright when I wasn't. The truth was, I was empty, and I was hurting and needed somebody to come and see about me. When you truly get sick and tired of being tired, you will seek after something better. What had been my comfort was no longer comforting to me. I needed more. Throwing another pity party wasn't going to work this time. I needed more. I was tired of people beating up on me, and I was tired of beating up on myself. I needed more. In that one moment, my life changed. When you make the step and own that what you've been doing hasn't worked, you open the door for opportunity, and help will come. I was at that point. I had to do something. I couldn't live another day feeling like this. Not knowing one day from the next, living from one place to the next, accepting handouts, and then having people talk about me. I had to do something. I did the only thing that I knew to do; I cried out for the first time in a long time. I called out to God, and I asked Him to help me. I told God how sorry I was and that I needed Him to make a way for me. I told Him that I did not want to die this way. I owned everything that I had done to get me to the place that I was, and I asked for forgiveness from the people that I had hurt along the way. I truly cried out to the Father. As I cried out to him, there was something that just kept saying, pick up the phone, dial the number, and she will answer. This was during one of the many times I moved back to the Carolina's to find myself, as I would put it. I hadn't talked to my sister in over a year, so I hesitated for a minute, but that voice was so clear, and it repeated the same message. When we are seeking for answers, you have to be still and listen for the voice of God. Don't question what you're hearing; that is, if you know the voice that you are listening to. The bible says that my sheep know my voice and a stranger they will not hear. I knew this voice all too well. Do what you're instructed to do. At first, I hesitated. This was the same person who had helped me out before, and I kept letting her down. This was the same person who stopped answering my calls and shut me out. Call Who? However, I picked up that phone and dialed the number, and she answered on the second ring I wish I could say that the turning point in my life came suddenly, but it didn't. Things got worse before they got better. I was determined that this would be my last spiral and that I was planting myself on solid ground. I had to go through hell before I got to this point. I sank into a deep depression. I didn't think well of myself and what I had become. I was broken. I was broken and shattered. I was living in a shell. Therapy didn't work for me. What good was therapy when, after leaving therapy, I went back out into the same distort world built around me? I got to the point where I decided that I didn't want to live. My family had already closed the door on me, so I decided that they wouldn't miss me, and life would be better without me. You see, this is what the enemy aims to do. He knows that if he can get into your mind and attack you there, the rest will be easy. You have to protect what you listen to and what you choose to believe. I didn't want to live but I was too scared to end my life also. I knew the word and I knew what choosing to end my life would mean for my eternity.

I may not have been living the principles, but I knew them. I started drinking even more. Remember, this was the only comfort that I knew that worked.

The more I drank, the less I felt.

Needless to say, I was killing myself very slowly. I think that my turning point was having someone look at me one day and told me, "Neicy, you know what people are saying about you? They're saying that you don't have anything going for yourself."

After saying what they said, they looked at me as though they expected me to respond. My response was, I walked away. I know that's not what they expected me to do, but that was all I had at that moment. What was I to say when they were right. When I was alone later that night, of course I thought about what was said and reality set in. It was all true. I really didn't have anything going for myself, at least that's what the enemy wanted me to believe.

There came that moment when I realized that what I had been doing was not living but existing.

I had honestly forgotten what life was all about. It all came back to putting on that mask and pretending that I was okay. This time I couldn't just put on the mask. Putting on the mask was not an option for me this time. I was tired of pretending that I was alright when I wasn't. The truth was, I was empty, and I was hurting and needed somebody to come and see about me. When you genuinely get sick and tired of being tired, you will seek after something better. What had been my comfort was no longer comforting to me. I needed more. Throwing another pity party wasn't going to work this time. I needed more. I was tired of people beating up on me, and I was tired of beating up on myself. I needed more. At that one moment, my life changed. When you make the step and own that what you've been doing hasn't worked, you open the door for opportunity, and help will come. I was at that point. I had to do something. I couldn't live another day feeling like this. Not knowing one day from the next, living from one place to the next, accepting handouts, and then having people talk about me. I had to do something. I did the only thing that I knew to do; I cried out for the first time in a long time. I called out to God, and I asked Him to help me. I told God how sorry I was and that I needed Him to make a way for me. I said to Him that I did not want to die this way.

I owned everything that I had done to get me to the place I was, and I asked for forgiveness from the people I had hurt along the way. I honestly cried out to the Father. As I cried out to him, there was something that just kept saying, pick up the phone, dial the number, and she will answer. This was during one of the many times I moved back to the Carolina's to find myself, as I would put it. I hadn't talked to my sister in over a year, so I hesitated for a minute, but that voice was so clear, and it repeated the same message.

When we are seeking answers, you have to be still and listen for the voice of God. Don't question what you're hearing; that is if you know the voice that you are listening to. The bible says that my sheep know my voice and a stranger they will not hear. I knew this voice all too well. Do what you're instructed to do. At first, I hesitated. This was the same person who had helped me out before, and I kept letting her down. This was the same person who stopped answering my calls and shut me out. Call Who? However, I picked up that phone and dialed the number, and she answered on the second ring. I was blown away. After a year of no communication, she answered this phone.

All I could say was, "Thank you, God!"

God is still in the prayer answering business. He did not leave me out here to die, and He hadn't forgotten about me. All I had to do was ask. A week later, I was reunited with my family. God had given me yet another chance. The enemy wants you to believe that once a failure, always a failure. That's a lie from the Pit of Hell, and you need to rebuke that spirit and cast it back into the pit from whence it came. I had been at this place before. Of course, doubt rose in me. Whenever those feelings rose, I had to remember from whence I came. Coming back was the easy part. I had to figure out how this time was going to be different from any other time. I had to figure out why I kept making the same bad choices over and over again.

There were more questions than I had answers to. I didn't know what I was going to do, but I knew that whatever I was going to do, it had to work this time. There was no going back.

I started to get back on my feet. Finding a job was the easy part. Finding direction and finding what I was supposed to do with the rest of my life was the next step. I guess I had been back in Delaware for about two months. All I could think about was my church family. I was too embarrassed to go back to church when I got back, so I streamed the services from home. That's another trick that the enemy threw my way. I believed that the way I left, my church family wouldn't want to have anything to do with me either. Don't let the enemy play you like that. He will try to convince you that nobody cares and that you are all alone.

I remember after streaming a service, I in-boxed my Bishop and told him I was back and how embarrassed I was and that I had been streaming the services. It wasn't long before he inboxed me back and told me to come home and that the church would always be my family. Isn't that just like a father? I felt like the prodigal son going back home. I got back on my feet. It was a struggle, but I was determined. Things were different this time.

Before, I was dependent on my sister. This time, she backed off, and I had to take on the responsibility of my life. There were times that I got angry with her and couldn't believe she wasn't going to help me out. I am so glad that she pushed me out there, and I had to become self-sufficient. It's easy to ride on someone else's coat tail. It feels even better when you make it on your own. As the songwriter says, "Papa may have. Mama may have, but God bless the child that's got his own." I was in a good place. I still had some struggles. This was not going to be an easy journey, and there were several bumps in the road. I still had my connections in the Carolina's and for a while, I kept going back. I didn't know what a stronghold was at this time, but now that I know, I understand why I kept going back to the same old routines. A stronghold is an idea, a thought process, a habit, or an addiction through which the enemy has set up occupancy in your life--a place where he has the advantage.

This process of going back to what I felt comfortable with, although I knew it wasn't good for me, was a definite stronghold. I listened to all the messages in church and made all the vows to leave the past behind. I did for a while, but eventually, I always went back. It's easy to say what we will or will not do, especially when things are going well in our lives. It's those times when loneliness, discouragement, and when things just aren't going the way you had planned. That's when your faith is being tested. Those are the times that you have to remember why you're doing what you're doing, and you push past those feelings. You have to choose to believe in something, or you will fall for anything. One Sunday, after hearing a message in church, I finally got it. There can be no reconciliation until you surrender it all.

You have to decide to leave it all behind. Up until this time, I haven't mentioned a lot about spirituality. There is a reason for that. Up until this point, I believed in God. I was born again, and I had a relationship with Him. However, although I knew God, I hadn't completely put my trust in Him. I was still trying to do things my way. I still believed that I could have a life with Him, but I could also hold on to parts of my old life. How wrong was I. Remember when I said that you have to close the door to some things? I wasn't ready to do all that. That's why I kept going back. Every time I went back to visit, I came back feeling more defeated. It would take me weeks to get myself back together. I couldn't understand why I felt the way I did. I know the answer now. You can't mix old and new together. The pieces just don't connect. It's like mixing oil and water. I had to understand that what I needed to do was close the backdoor. I had cleaned up my life and was moving forward, but I still left the backdoor open for the past to enter. The other thing I had to do was delete some numbers. Yeah, that was the hard part. How could I delete the numbers of people that I had known all my life?

This was family and friendships formed over a lifetime, and I was expected to hit delete on them. You have to understand that there will come a time in life that you have got to travel this road alone. It goes back to who you are listening to and what you want out of life. It doesn't matter whether it's family or friends. If they aren't making a positive impact on your life, hit "delete." So, I had to close those doors and delete those numbers.

I had to say "NO" to some invitations and change places that I went. I couldn't talk to some people.

I had to want this new life. I heard this saying, "Don't keep looking back in the rearview mirror; you may stay too long." I had to take that on for a while. I couldn't look back. I couldn't entertain thoughts of yesterday, or those feelings would arise. You have to understand where you are in your journey.

You may not be ready for the family reunions. You have to do what you need to do without thinking about what others may feel about it.

I had to keep pressing my way and tune people out. I had listened to people for long enough. I had to understand that this was my journey, and I had to walk it out. I had been dependent for so long. I was dependent on my mother, my sister, husband, this person, and that, and now it was time to be dependent on me. It hurt for a while, and sometimes the pain tried to come back, but I had to give it up. There comes that moment when you just have to step out there and do it. You can't think about it too long, or you'll start to second guess yourself. I had second-guessed myself so many times until I didn't trust my judgment, but I made a decision this time to just go for it.

I had committed in my heart that failure was not an option and that if I fell down, I wasn't going to stay down.

Did the enemy try to test me? Of course, he did and still does. I just don't give up as easily as I had in the past.

I also learned that this doesn't have to be a journey that you travel all alone. I had to surround myself with people who had positive attitudes. One reason I kept failing was because of the company that I was entertaining. When all you hear is negative, you start to think negatively, and negative becomes normal and acceptable to you. Because I had trust issues, this wasn't easy for me.

The more I started to fellowship with people of the same faith, the more I understood that not everyone was out to get me. These people helped me to realize that my life was important and that I did matter.

At first, I was skeptical of why they would care about me. I thought that they had a hidden agenda, and so I was very standoffish. I didn't allow myself to get close to people, and I didn't allow them to get close to me. They didn't give up on me, and I'm grateful that they didn't. They taught me about hope, and they taught me faith.

I remember going to the altar one Sunday morning to come back in right standing with the church. As I was standing at the front of the church, I remember hearing through my tears, Bishop Haskell saying, "He didn't leave you out there to die." It was as if God himself was talking to me.

As I pondered on those words, all I could think about was my life. It was as if I were watching a movie of my life play out in front of me. All the hurt that I had been through and all the pain that I felt, He did not leave me out there to die. To that, all I could say was, "God, I thank you." There had been so much drama in my life, but through all that drama and the mess I had been through, some not my fault, and some of it was my fault; through all of that, God still kept me. He still had a covering over me. Thank God for grace and mercy. I now know that it was God's grace that covered me to this point. I still stumble, and I still mess up, but God's grace keeps me. Through all of my fears, tears, doubts, failures, and victories,

I know that I owe it all to Him. When I could have given up, and for the times that I did give up, He was always there standing by me even though at the moment I couldn't feel it. I know now that all that was not to kill me but to build character and develop and prepare me for this moment. No matter what you're going through, remember you are not alone. As the songwriter says: "He walks with me and He talks with me. He tells me that I am His own." Sometimes that's what you have to do. You have to steal away to the garden, your secret place, and bask in His glory. You have to find your war room. That's where your journey begins. Prayer is the key to everything. Through prayer, you will make it through this journey. You may be broken right now. You may not know which direction to go. The struggle has been real, and this is not just in your mind. You are in a battle but remember the battle is not yours to fight. It belongs to God. You have to be willing to reach out for help. You have carried this burden too long alone. Open your heart and be receptive that

God has placed people in your life to help you find your purpose in life. I wish I had reached out earlier in my own life. I'm convinced that I would have saved myself so much pain. I walked outside of my purpose for so long because I didn't want to admit that I didn't have the answers, and I didn't know how to reach out and ask for help. You don't have to stay broken. There is healing for your soul. You have got to keep pressing your way.

Paul says, "I press toward the mark of the high calling." Failure is not an option. You have been in this dark pit for too long. It's time to take steps to come out of this darkness and walk in your purpose. When I started this journey, I didn't know what purpose or destiny was, but I sought to find out what purpose was and what I needed to do to find it. My former pastor, Pastor Monica Haskell, taught a class on "Finding your Purpose." The dictionary defines purpose as the reason for which something exists. As I began to think about this definition, I started to ask myself, why do I exist, and why am I here? I had been through a lot, and in my natural mind, I shouldn't be here. The more I studied purpose, the more I wanted to know what mine was. After doing an introspective look at my life, I began to look back over the things that I had gone through, and I began to understand that there was a reason for all of this. All of this was to prepare me to walk in purpose.

God started revealing my purpose to me. It didn't just happen like that, but I gradually began to understand.

When I found purpose, I began to run from it. I didn't want to accept it, and I couldn't believe God had chosen me for this assignment. God has shown me that all I have gone through was witnessing what God can do through brokenness. My past consists of hurt, betrayal, abuse, and wrong choices. My purpose is to let you know that where you've come from does not define who you're meant to be. There is hope. I want to let you know there is life past the pain and that you can still have that life you deserve. You can still have a fulfilled life. Don't let your setbacks hold you back from a future that God wants for you and has designed for you. I remember hearing my pastor say that you should write your vision. Here was something else new to me. Now that I had found purpose, I needed to know what vision was. I remember Bishop Haskell asking the question: "Where do you see yourself in the future?" Here we go with something else that I had to ponder. I had never really given much thought to the future. Until then, I didn't know that there was a future out there for me.

I was still trying to make it through each day. Vision is defined as the ability to see or picture in your mind what you wish to pursue.

Again, I had no idea what this was all about. For so long, I had walked in darkness, and now I had to think outside of the darkness.

What was out there waiting for me?

I had to learn how to dream again.

Then I learned about the vision board.

You need to be able to see your dreams.

That's the vision board's purpose to use as a tool to inspire you to move toward your new life. Paul says, "Write the vision." Make it a group project and host "vision parties" to help inspire your friends. This is a good way to start seeing your dreams while helping others see their vision as well.

The Bible teaches us that we were created for a divine purpose.

Before we were formed in the womb, God had a purpose with you in mind. Although this wonderful life is out there for us, He also gave us a free choice. He gives us free will. We all have choices to make in our lives. We can either follow the path that He has designed that leads to a fulfilled life, or we can choose to walk in our path and struggle throughout life. Healing doesn't come as a quick fix. It's a process. Setbacks come, but you have to push your way through. In your healing, remember you don't have to walk this road alone. Put God first, and he will direct you in the way that you should go. It won't

always be the way you choose, but during these times, you have to trust God. I know now that if I had put my trust in God at the beginning, I would have saved myself a lot of heartaches and surely a lot of pain. Even though it's important to speak over your own life, surrounding yourself with positive people is a must. A person with no dream of their own definitely can't be supportive of your dreams. You need people to encourage you not to have pity parties with you. Always remember you are your own best friend. You can't control how other people think and feel. Take care of yourself. Deal with your issues, and God will restore you to the woman of God you were created to be. You can be restored. To God be the glory!!! God is always with you. He has been from the very beginning. It's by His grace and mercy that you have made it this far. He didn't bring you this far to leave you now. He has covered you and will continue to walk with you through it all. Do you trust Him? Do you really trust Him? Seek God and tell Him your heart's desires. Cry out unto the Lord. He is waiting for you. What do you have to lose?

CHAPTER 5

Mending Broken Relationships

We experience many types of relationships during our lives. Whether the relationship is family, friends, personal or intimate, the way we approach our relationships are very crucial if they are going to be successful. Any relationship that has been formed takes time, and when that relationship has been damaged, it takes even more time to mend them. Many relationships don't last because we don't want to take the time to devote time to them. Most of the time, we feel this way because of the past relationships that we spent too much time on and benefited nothing from them. When we're building relationships, you must first factor in whether this will be productive or counterproductive to where you are trying to go in life. Is it worth investing your time into the relationship? Any good relationship is based on what you put into it. The harder you work on them, the stronger the bond becomes. For these relationships to be successful, it's important to move the clutter from your life. People who are trying to succeed in life don't have time to deal with clutter and drama.

Another thing is not to jump back into or form relationships based on feelings. Sometimes your feelings can lead you down the wrong path. The majority of my relationships were based on how I was feeling at the time. I thought that I was always good at judging people's character. I have often heard that first impressions are lasting impressions. The one thing that I valued myself for was forming opinions about people within minutes of meeting them. Of course, most of the time, my first opinions were wrong. I always try not to prejudge; however, I do firmly believe that the more time you spend with a person, their true colors, and their true motives will come to the surface. I'm not saying that you should be like a watchdog waiting for something to go wrong but what's inside usually comes out, whether good or bad. I've learned that it's alright to ask questions.

These are the people that you're letting into your life, hopefully for the long haul. Of course, I can say all this easily now. That has not always been the case. I jumped into relationships, whether they were friendships, business, or personal head first, and I wore my heart on my sleeve, exposing too much.

How do-good relationships form and last? While researching this topic, I found that all relationships come about because we all have particular needs that we want to be fulfilled, whether it be physical, mental, emotional, or social. If the needs that we want aren't fulfilled, the relationship will most likely not last. The purpose of establishing relationships is to make us feel good. What often happens in pursuing these relationships is that we attempt to squeeze happiness out of the other individual and do the same to us, which often causes a battle. When you look at it, it all makes sense. How can you give someone else what you don't have for yourself? As Michael Jackson would say, "Look at that man in the mirror," before trying to judge someone else. I think that is what happened in the majority of my relationships that caused them to fail. I was so busy looking at others and trying to find fault in them and what they couldn't do for me when I should have reversed the question and asked what part I played in not fulfilling the void that the other person needed to be filled?

Many of our relationships fail because we expect what we can't give. Often, we pursue relationships to not only fill our desires but to fill in the gaps of our own lives. We feel that urge just to have someone on our side to complete us instead of finding other ways to fill those gaps.

Another reason many of our relationships fail is that we fail to communicate. We don't take the time to listen to others, whether it be our children, husbands, friends, family, significant others, or our associates.

We hear what they say, but we don't listen to understand the why's of what they are saying. We all have an agenda in conversation and the idea that what we have to say is more important. We want to be heard and understood but don't offer the same to others. Listening to understand is crucial. Honestly, that was not my strong point in any relationship that I have had. It was not at the front of what I had to achieve. I wanted to be heard, and really, that's all I wanted. I wasn't talking for anyone to give me feedback. I just wanted you to know what was on my mind at the time. That was it, and it was a setup for failure from the beginning. I have since learned to slow down and listen to what others have to say. Open communication is the only way good relationships will last. I had to learn to listen without interruption and not judge intentionally. It was hard for me to do, and it took time for me to get it. I always felt the need to interject my opinion. When I learned to stop and listen, I found that people responded better, and my opinions were received and appreciated.

Relationships are based on trust. This was another area that I had difficulty. My experience with trusting people in the past ended with me being hurt, especially in romantic relationships. My problem again was running off of feelings. I wore my heart on my sleeve, and I accepted what was given openly and easily because I needed to believe in something and someone.

It was as though people could see through me and see the need to be accepted and used it to their advantage.

The fact that I had very low self-esteem didn't help either. I was very vulnerable when it came to relationships. I needed things to fair well for me, so I had to believe. That's where knowing you and loving yourself comes into play. If you don't believe in yourself and love yourself, you will fall for anything.

It's essential to spend time with yourself before seeking out relationships. Until you know what you want and expect out of a relationship, leave it alone. If you don't, you'll end up making bad relationship decisions making your life and the people around you miserable as well. However, when you are ready to pursue those relationships, trust is required.

Without trust, you will never be free to enjoy the person/persons you're in relationships. Without trust, you will always be worrying or thinking about what the other person is doing when they're not with you or what they're saying about you. I sabotaged many good relationships because of trust issues of the past. When I found people that were there for me, really there for me, I questioned their motives, and I tried to control the relationship, which ended with those people eventually giving up on the relationship and moving on. There also has to be honesty in any relationship for it to be successful. Be truthful of your expectations from the relationship. Don't leave others guessing, and don't try to convince them that you want the same things that they want. For you to be honest with them, you must first be honest with yourself. I had to learn this, as well.

It was hard for me to tell what I wanted from a relationship. I didn't know what I wanted because I didn't have any expectations to share. I never even gave it any thought until I was in an actual relationship and realized what I didn't want. Through time, I realized after doing the introspective look in the mirror and time with myself that I did have expectations and things that I did want out of life. Not expressing what you want or need leads to disappointment, but at least it gives the other person a fighting chance. I also learned to stop being so "needy." I felt that I gave of myself so freely, and people took advantage of that in the past. So, I learned to be selfish.

I took on the perception of "what's in it for me?" I had always been a giver, and it cost me. I flipped the script and went from being a "giver" to a "taker." I developed a mindset that it was my turn, and I was going to get mine. That didn't work out well for me. You can't keep taking things from a relationship and never put anything into it. My problem was that I had given for so long and had given so much that I didn't feel that I had anything else to give. What I didn't understand was that I had so much more to give. There was so much more than I had to offer to people. When I started making time for these people and gave them my time and attention, I found that it was worth more than money or any material gift.

Those were the gifts that mattered to the real people in my life. I also learned that everything that I said or everything that I did was not always right. It was hard to accept because I wanted to be right in everything. I wanted people to believe that I knew what was best and that I had to believe that I was under control. I had been wrong for so long. I needed to be right. Fact is, with all the stuff that I had been through, I didn't know "jack."

Being right feels good. Everybody wants to feel good. No one wants to feel bad for themselves. My problem in my relationships was that I didn't like to be told what to do, and in some cases, rightly so. In others, I needed guidance, and I rejected it, and I later paid the price for it. I am learning to let go of that need to be right as I continue to grow. I'm learning through growth and maturity to understand that other people have opinions, too, and that's okay. I have learned, just as I want to be accepted, whether right or wrong, others feel the same way. Now, I look at building relationships positively, seeing the good in people, and accepting that not everyone is out to get me. I am open to being optimistic and having a positive outlook.

When I took on this outlook, I began to form trusting, honest and loving relationships that were long overdue.

You have got to let the past be the past. You have to let those unhealthy relationships stay buried. If you don't, you will never find the positive relationships that you so desire. You have to become vulnerable and open yourself up. Staying in your comfort zone will only leave you feeling lonely and depressed. Some people genuinely care about you. If you never open the door, you will never experience what they have to offer you and what you have to offer to them. You will always have disappointments in your life. It's what you do during those times that change the course of your life. I think the thing that kept me back so long was that I wanted to believe that none of the hurt or disappointments that afflicted me were intentional. I couldn't ponder in my mind why anyone who said they loved and cared for me would ever want to hurt me. It became easier to follow the course and to believe that it was all me. People will always disappoint you. Don't put all your eggs into one basket. You have to know who your star players are, and you have to know how far in the game are they willing to go and when is the right time to discard some of those players and replace them with some loyal players who stick until the game is over.

My mistake was believing that every one of my players was there until the end. However, I realized that the only time they were in the game was when it was convenient and beneficial on their behalf. When I was at my high, friends were plentiful. It was when I hit my lowest point that I found out who was true.

When I was broke and busted, no one could be found, and those who were around stuck to tell me how I messed up and

how I was at fault for whatever was going on. Some stuck it out with me. I have to give credit where credit is due, and that number was few. You have to decide what's important to you. Is it more important to be liked for what you have to give to them, or is it more important to have people in your life who legitimately care about you and what's going on in your life? Sometimes you have got to know when to just let it go. You have to know when it's time to close the door to those negative relationships. It doesn't matter the length of time for the relationship. Whenever the relationship is no longer beneficial for the course you have set for yourself; it is time to close that chapter of your life. Who wants to be around negativity all the time? Remember, everyone doesn't want to see you succeed in life. The sooner you realize this for yourself, the better off you will be. You also need to be wary of the associations you have with people who always try to make you feel guilty for wanting better for your life. Close the door to negativity. If you keep the door open, you're inviting all the unwanted drama to come in and reside. The thing that I feared the most was what to do after I closed the door. I was afraid of being alone, not realizing that I was already alone anyway. I stayed in some of those unhealthy relationships for so long because of that fear and paid a hefty price for hanging on for so long. Another reason I hung in for so long was because I felt obligated to some of those same people. I was made to feel as though I owed them, and to close the door to them would be an insult or a slap to the face. Don't let people back you into that corner with the constant reminders of what they did for you back then. Remember what I said to you earlier on. The enemy does not care who he has to use to bring you down. Take the focus off of what you failed at. Make the decision to stop looking at where you came from and put the focus on who you want to become and where you want to go. Stop using your life as a scapegoat for why you're where you're at. You have to push past that and put all that behind you. For every problem, there is a solution. For every negative, there is a positive. It's time to stop feeling sorry for yourself.

You can't stay down when you fall. I still stumble, and I still fall short. Take some of that negative energy and turn it into a positive. You don't have to face life alone. That's a choice. Seek out people who have been where you are and made it back. There is help out there for the asking. You have to reach out and grab those opportunities.

You have to realize that there is help out there. There are people waiting for you to reach out. You have to remember that not everyone is out there to get you. When it's all said and done, remember this, all the help in the world will not help you if you don't stay focused. At the end of the day, it's all up to you. It's time to make some choices. Stop procrastinating. The time is now. You can't wait another day. You have everything you need within you to move forward. There is life after the pain. Be confident in knowing that life is not based on the mistakes of the past. Life is only over when you make a choice to give up, or you make a choice to stay where you are. I can't stress enough how important it is to surround yourself with positive people. Seek out these people. They have been where you are trying to go and are willing to share those experiences with you. It's not going to jump in your lap. You have to seek it out. Find a mentor. Be wise in seeking out a mentor. Make sure that you have a revelation on this is a relationship you want to pursue.

Experience is the best teacher you will ever encounter. Mentors have that experience, and partnering with someone with this experience under their belt is a plus. It can keep you from making some horrible mistakes that will keep you from reaching your destiny or cause a delay in you getting where you need to be. None of this can come about if you don't come out from behind those walls you have built around you. You have to be willing to meet people and again make yourself vulnerable. Don't just presume that people know what you need. The only way someone can know what you need is if you seek out help. Build those relationships. Come out of that pit. It's time to move forward. It's time to let the past be the past. No longer is it acceptable to let the past determine who you are and who you hope to become. Move forward. Destiny awaits you.

CHAPTER 6
Building Relationships

The hardest thing that I have had to come to grips with was forgiving those who have harmed me along the way. I didn't understand how harboring anger, bitterness, resentfulness, and hate were holding me back from moving forward to destiny for my life.

How was I expected just to let go of all the feelings that had built up on the inside of me after years of hurt, disappointment, and abuse? I didn't understand how or why I was expected to forgive people that hurt me. This was not something that happened once or twice but repeatedly over the years, yet I was expected to forgive all this bitterness that had become a part of my life. Being bitter had become who I was. It was a part of me so much that it overtook me. I found myself walking around with all these walls surrounding me.

I learned to pretend that I was okay and that nothing that was done to me affected me. I wore masks for years. I thought that no one could see my pain, and I smiled and lied my way through each day. When I was alone, and the masks were off, I looked into the mirror, the person I saw looking back at me I didn't recognize.

I saw a shadow of a person who had been beaten, torn down, stomped on, dismissed, and defeated. Soon the masks didn't work anymore if they ever did work. I didn't realize that the more I held my anger inside, it grew and would one day

show its ugly face. One day the masks were unveiled, and people started to come to me, even my daughter and asked why I always looked angry as though the weight of the whole world were on my shoulder. What they didn't understand was I didn't feel as though I had anything to smile about. I became angrier because I felt judged. I didn't feel that anyone had the right to tell me how I was supposed to look or feel.

They didn't know what I was carrying inside, and at the time, I felt as though the world's weight was on my shoulder. I dare they judge me was all I kept saying to myself. Really, the majority of the time, I didn't realize that I had a frown on my face. I was just looking like me, I thought. I try not to be confrontational with people, so even though I was thinking these thoughts, I kept them to myself and walked around with my head down and kept those feelings buried inside me.

Now I understand that some confrontations can be beneficial. We talked about the lack of communication being the main reason for broken relationships in the previous chapter. How is anyone to know what's on your mind unless you tell them? If you never tell someone that something they said or did hurt or offended you, how are they to respond? When you don't communicate your feelings, they end up festering on the inside and what goes in is what will come out. It's all a matter of time. By the time the roof blows off, the situation is out of control. What could have been an innocent mistake or lack of judgment is now an all-out catastrophe. My problem was, I didn't feel that I should have been expected to inform anyone that something they did or said offended me. If you knew me, you would have thought of the outcome before you did or said it. In some incidences, this was true. The act was intentional. I was the one who was offended, and now I have to seek a resolution. I didn't think so. The bible says that if a brother offends you, you should go to that brother and work it out. I know you might say that's biblical, but we live in the real world.

Same God, same answer, you should go if, for no other reason, The Heavenly Father says so. When you have committed yourself to this stage in the game, you must have a full understanding of what forgiveness entails.

To forgive is defined as to stop feeling angry or resentful toward someone for an offense, flaw, or mistake. It means to cancel a debt. There are many scriptures in the Bible that speak on forgiveness. One of God's commandments is that we forgive our brothers as He has forgiven us. My biggest problem was when it said that if the offense was reoccurring, we are to forgive each time they ask for forgiveness if it were a genuine apology.

I couldn't grasp how I was expected to do this. My real struggle was the fact that, in all honesty, I didn't want to forgive. I wanted revenge and for them to suffer and hurt the same as I had or worse. I didn't understand how important forgiveness was to my destiny. Luke 17:3-4 says, "Without forgiveness, there is no hope." We fail to understand that when we refuse to forgive, we hold back our blessings. God will not bless an unforgiving heart. The more I learned about forgiveness, the more I struggled with it.

True forgiveness is not easy to do.

I had often said that I had forgiven someone when I hadn't. I spoke the words, but my actions said something totally different. I was still stiff-lip and held a grudge in my heart. Whenever the subject arose, I was quick to bring up the wrong that was done to me. The more I dwelt on the hurt and pain, the less forgiving I became. I didn't realize that I wasn't hurting anybody by not forgiving, but I was doing an injustice to myself physically and emotionally. It took too much energy to hold onto all the anger and grudges than to let it go and move on with life. When we choose to hold onto hurt and pain, really that's all you're doing is hurting you.

God tells us to forgive. That's it. He didn't say that we had to continue to be in a relationship with the individual. He said to forgive. Another area I had difficulty in was asking for forgiveness. I had trouble in this area because I hadn't owned my responsibility for the wrongs that I had done. I hurt a lot of people during my struggles. I caused pain to people who truly didn't deserve what I had put them through. Because of the place that I was in during the time, I couldn't see that. The only person I could see that had been wronged was me. When I did come to grips and started owning my mess, I didn't know how to ask for forgiveness. Some of the pain I had caused was deep, and I didn't know how to fix my wrongs. What I learned later was that it wasn't for me to fix.

On my own, I would have made it worse.

The first thing you need to do when seeking forgiveness is to seek direction from the Holy Spirit. Seek Him for guidance and listen for an answer.

Ensure your motives for asking for forgiveness are pure and not just to make you feel less guilty. That's not how it works. Once I sought direction through prayer and scriptures, it prepared me to go to specific individuals, and their response towards me was far greater than I could ever imagine. To be honest, there were those individuals that I didn't want to ask for forgiveness out of human nature. I truly believed that I had done no wrong and that I was a victim. However, I did what was required of me. When you go to someone, and they don't forgive you, move on. What they do with the apology is on them. They are responsible for what they do.

I had convinced myself that the hardest thing I had to do was to forgive others. I soon came to realize that this was not necessarily true. Not in my case anyway. The hardest thing that I have yet to encounter throughout this whole journey is forgiving myself. This is the area that I struggle with even to this day. It was hard forgiving others from my past. It was even harder asking others to forgive me. The hardest thing I have encountered was forgiving myself for letting myself down and those I love. Those years that I was wandering around doing my own thing, fulfilling my selfish desires, hurt many people. During those times, all I could think about was me and what I wanted out of life. I was very self-centered, and I was my agenda, and it didn't matter at the time who stood in my way. I never imagined the pain I was putting my loved ones through.

That's often the case when we succumb to the pressures of life. You don't consider the feelings of others because it interferes with your agenda and what you think you want out of life, not realizing the hurt you're causing or how

it will come back and affect your

life in the future. Once I got on the right path to getting my life back under control, I could see clearly, and what I saw I didn't like. I couldn't believe, nor did I want to believe, that I had caused all this pain that I had inflicted on them. When it all came to light, I was first in denial and convinced myself that this was all made up, and the situations were dramatized to make me out to be the bad guy. I convinced myself that this was a ploy to make me feel guilty for living my life the way I chose. Then I became angry and took everything personally because I convinced myself that because I was happy and their lives were not going the way they thought they should,

they blamed me for their unhappiness.

Then came the hurt and the acceptance that this was all me, and I had caused this pain, and I had to admit how selfish I had been and that I was only concerned about myself. When it got to this point, I went into a state of depression.

No matter what I had done in life, I never intentionally meant to hurt anyone, but I did.

At this point, I was at my lowest.

Without the alcohol clouding my mind, everything was put into perspective, and at times it became overwhelming to the point that I didn't want to go on with life. I didn't feel as though I deserved to move on with life. It was surreal. I had made a mess out of my life. The mess was so grave that even though I tried to mend some broken relationships, they couldn't be mended. Those that did forgive me; I didn't feel worthy of their forgiveness. I had crushed them with my selfishness. I abandoned those who loved me the most, yet they were there with open arms when I came to my senses. How could I move on after what I had done? I felt guilty, and I felt as though everything that I had gone through, I deserved.

It was my punishment for all the wrong I committed and all the hurt that I had caused. I spent a lot of time dwelling on the hurt that I had caused.

I couldn't move past the pain.

People that loved me and fought for me even when I was wrong, I let them down. I walked away from them when they tried to help me, and the things I said and my actions toward them disgusted me, and I became disgusted with myself. Who had I become? I didn't know this person, and I didn't want to. Then my guilt led to shame. Shame is different from guilt. Shame causes you to feel inferior, inadequate and makes you feel bad versus regretting what you did in feeling guilt. The shame that I carried on the inside lowered my self-esteem even more. I had to learn that continuing to beat up on myself only prolonged my guilt and my shame.

I walked around with my head down, and my esteem was damaged. It was only when I accepted responsibility for my actions and owned up to what I had done that my life changed for the better. It comes down to once again; you have to own the wrong that you have done. You can't keep pushing it to the rear. It's true that what's done in the dark will come to light. You can't walk around pretending that everything will work out on its own if you just leave it alone. It doesn't work like that either. When you acknowledge the wrong you have done and ask yourself for forgiveness, you're taking the right steps to restore. You can't just say that you have forgiven yourself; you have to truly believe and accept the forgiveness and promise not to make the same mistakes again. It's a process within itself. Always remember that you are not in this alone. You are responsible for making the first step, and the first step is learning to forgive yourself and move from the past. Forgiving means not looking back. You can't keep looking back and dwelling on the mistakes of the past.

Move forward with your life and leave all that pain behind you. Is it easy?

No. No one said that it would be. Like everything else worth having, you have to work on it and make it a daily confession. There are some things that you can do to help you in the forgiving process. Try writing yourself a letter expressing your understanding and appreciation of forgiveness.

Tell yourself daily that you are forgiven and that your life is worth something. Think about what you did and what you learned from it and think of ways to make amends with those you hurt. It's important to realize that you can forgive yourself and accept that you were at fault in the same way that you forgive someone else though you think they are wrong. You can't keep regretting what you did yet accept that you're human, and we all mess up and make mistakes. Forgiving yourself doesn't mean not being angry with yourself but learning not to hate yourself. Also, it is important to understand why you need to forgive yourself.

Remember, we don't need to be forgiven for being human, and we don't need to be forgiven for being who we are.

Sometimes we confuse forgiveness with condoning our actions or a lack of accountability. Forgiveness is about relinquishing a source of pain and letting go of the resentment. We sometimes look at self-forgiveness as letting ourselves get away with something. That's a scapegoat. Self-forgiveness is truly being resentful for the wrong that we have done. You truly know that you have forgiven yourself when the memory gives you no more pain. When the subject comes up, and you don't get all riled up and bitter. You know that you have truly forgiven when you can say, "I'm free of this," and you feel less burdened and start to feel good about yourself. Remember this; it's okay for you to move forward and there is help out there. Don't walk around with this guilt and shame for the remainder of your life. You will never walk-in purpose, holding onto the past. You have to let it go. Reach out.

People do care about you, whether you believe it or not. Not everyone has given up on you, and don't you dare give up on yourself. Tell yourself that I've carried this burden long enough. I've let this thing control me long enough. Search yourself and ask the Holy Spirit for guidance. Talk to somebody. Break the bondage of feeling burdened and weighed down. We have all been there, and we have all messed up.

Look at forgiveness as pressing the reset button on life. Get ready to push the reset button and take the second chance in life. There is power in forgiveness. Release the power and get ready to step into your destiny.

CHAPTER 7

Moving Forward

No matter what background you may have come from or what hardships you may have encountered, there is a purpose for you being here on this earth that was designed specifically with you in mind. No matter what you have experienced in life, we all have something, a reason that we get up each day and keep it moving. Despite the obstacles in our paths, we keep going despite the disappointments and setbacks. This reason is called "purpose."

As I said earlier, I didn't know what the word purpose meant or how it pertained to my life. I was once asked the question, "Do you know what your purpose in life is?" I was baffled at the question, but as the definition was clarified for me, it made me perplexed, and I needed to find out more about this thing called purpose.

For review, purpose is defined as the reason why something exists or why something is done. I still couldn't figure out what this had to do with me and what was going on in my life at the time. As I continued to think about this thing, I wanted to know the reason I existed. I had gone through a lot in my life, and naturally, I should not be here, but I am still here for some reason, and I needed to discover why? As I did an introspective look at my life, I started playing my life back in my mind. The more I looked back, the more I could see the why factor of my life and my existence on this earth. Some of what I saw was hard to relive, but I saw why looking back was so relevant to my future and where I was about to go in life. I saw the pain, hurt, betrayal, abuse, abandonment, fear, doubt, and distrust.

I saw more than I wanted to see.

I pondered this in my mind, and as I studied this thing called purpose, God revealed to me what my purpose was and why I'm still here. My purpose is to show others that I'm still here, even through all the hurt and pain. I'm stronger now than ever, and I have hope for a better future. My testimony of what I've been through is to be a witness of what God can do with a broken, shattered vessel, how He can mend the broken pieces back together and complete a new thing, a new creation, a vessel that can be used for His glory. He showed me that only through Him could this shattered and torn vessel be mended and put back together. I may be scarred, but I'm still usable. No therapy could do what God has done in my life. We put our trust in everyone else. We run to doctors, family, friends, and whoever will listen before seeking help from the only one who holds the answers. I'm not saying that it's wrong to seek help or advice from others, but when it comes down to being restored and being able to live a life with hope, there's only one who can put it all together, and that's the Creator Himself. Jeremiah 29: 11 says, "For I know the plans that I have for you says the Lord, they are plans for good and not for disaster, to give you a future and a hope." What a Mighty God we serve. Did you understand what He said? He says, "To give you a future and a hope." That by itself deserves a praise! It sums it all up. I remember when I didn't know what to expect day after day, and here this is saying to me that I have hope and a future.

That was overwhelming to me. I thought that could not be meant for me. I was too messed up, and who was I to think that I could have hope for anything. Then I learned about this thing called "vision." Again, I couldn't figure out how this would help me, but I was willing to listen and learn. I didn't know how this would help me get out of this messed-up life that I had created for myself but what the heck, how could it hurt. Vision is defined as the ability to see or picture in your mind what you want to pursue in life. That was easy. The only thing that I wanted from life was to make it to the next day. I didn't have a vision past that. All I knew was a life filled with gloom and shame. However, I started to think about life before I was messed up. I had dreams and goals that I wanted to achieve. I wasn't always in this dark place. I didn't like this place where I was. Could I get out? I wanted out.

I needed to have a dream again. I needed something that I could hold on to, something to believe. That's when I learned about the "vision board." Remember, the vision board's purpose is to have something that you can physically see to use as a tool to inspire you toward your journey in your new life. I started thinking about those dreams that I once had, and I sought guidance from people who had used the vision board to move into their purpose and led them into their destiny. I sought direction from God and how my dreams and goals fit into His purpose for me. I wanted to know how my purpose and how my dreams could be of service to others just like me. Paul says, "Write the vision and make it plain." The bible teaches us that we all were created for a divine purpose. Even before we were formed in the womb of our mothers, God had a purpose with you in mind.

Although God wants us to walk in the life that He has created for us, and the fact that He is in charge of our lives, He has given us the freedom to choose the path we want to follow.

We were created with free will, the ability to make choices, and we are responsible for our choices.

I know I've said this before, but the review is important. I didn't know if I was ready for all of this. I wanted it, but I wasn't sure if I had what it took to get to this life that God wanted me to have. I didn't feel worthy. I had messed up too many times, and I hurt so many people along the way. I tried to talk my way out of believing that I could have this extraordinary life that was being put before me. I ran for years, trying to escape this call that was on my life.

The further I tried to escape, the more this thing kept tugging at me. Your past does not define who you are. My purpose in life is to let women who come from a past similar as mine know that there is hope for you. My purpose is to let you know that there is life after the pain and that you can still obtain what you started to do in your life. Don't let your setbacks hold you back from a future that God wants for you. I asked God, why would you want me to open myself up to talk about the abuse that I went through, the abandonment that I felt, and the betrayal that I suffered from people who said they cared about me? God answered my questions. He showed me that someone needed to hear my story. There is someone out there that needs to know that you can make it out even though it looks like the odds are stacked against you.

There is someone that needs to know that though you are broken, you still have a purpose. Someone needs to know that I didn't give up, and I didn't just accept what life thought I wasn't worthy. I fought, and I fight each day. I fight to have this life that God says that I can have. He revealed to me, "That's why I chose you." Someone is waiting on you. Your testimony is someone's deliverance. Through my pain and brokenness is where I met God. It's where I met the Potter, and it's where the Potter put me back together.

You do matter, and the Potter wants to put you back together again. I know that this may seem like a lot, and it seems impossible to do. Believe me; I felt the same way. I didn't see how any of this would work. When I tell you, I didn't know anything about working the faith process. I believed, but there was so much more to the process. I listened, and I studied faith. I put the things that I heard in the messages that my Bishop and Pastor taught on faith, and I started working on the faith process. Pursuing purpose and trying to reach that place God is trying to take you is a process, and faith is part of the process. You have to believe, and you have to trust that everything that God says is true and that everything he promised will come to pass.

If you have not invited Him to come into your life, I invite you to do so. Having a personal relationship with the Father is the only way any of this is possible. You have to have a personal relationship with Him. How can you hear from him if you don't know Him? You may say that I'm not ready for this yet. You will never be ready on your own. I promise if you would invite the Savior in, your life will never be the same. I began to work through the process. It's not a magic formula that you wave a wand, and suddenly it appears. No, there is a process that you have to work on, and it takes time and effort. You can't sit back and wait for your purpose to appear or for this new life to fall into your lap. There is a process that you have to go through. Just as you start on the bottom of a stairwell, you climb one step at a time until you reach the top. In that same manner, moving into your set place is the same process. You can't jump or skip steps. You must respect the process one step at a time. There are no shortcuts. The process doesn't make the journey harder. It does prepare you for when you reach your destiny.

Let's be honest. If we were to get everything we wanted handed to us right now, the majority of people, including myself, would not be able to handle it. It wouldn't last. You have to move into a place of maturity to handle what the future has in store. I tried several times to skip the process, and I failed and ended back at the starting point and had to start the process again. We all need order in our lives. You have to become focused, and you have to prioritize your life. There are things and people that you will have to let go. I know that it sounds harsh, but it's reality. You are on a mission, and the mission you're on cannot have distractions or extra baggage. You've got to unclutter your life. Not everyone is meant to go along for the ride. It's not their destiny; it's yours.

When it gets rough, you have got to stay focused. There will be those times that you may get discouraged, respect the process, and have patience. It may seem like a long journey, but God is preparing you to face the challenges that will come when you get to where you want to go. Hang in there!! Be encouraged. You're going to get there. This is and has been an incredible journey for me. I haven't gotten to the place that I want to be yet, but I still work through the process. I haven't achieved all my goals, and I still have setbacks, but I'm hanging in there, and I'm still working the process of moving up the steps one day at a time. Savor the small victories along the way. Appreciate how far you have come.

Don't get comfortable there. You still have a way to go. That's what I tell myself. I celebrate the small victories and remind myself daily; you still have work to do. I'm not there yet, but as my Bishop would say, "I see my future, and it sure looks good."

I couldn't always say that. Be encouraged my sister. There is light at the end of the tunnel. Don't be moved by what it seems like. Don't be moved by how it feels. Only be moved by what you believe. You're going to make it—your life matters. There is a destiny out there with your name on it, and it awaits you. Become a destiny stalker and go after yours. You have tried everything else. How has that worked out for you? This is not the time for giving up. You don't have another moment to waste. Put everything that you have into finding your rightful place.

It's out there for you. Don't be discouraged, and please don't give up.

Push and then push some more. It may seem that you are at the end of your rope.

Don't let go of the rope. Grasp harder and pull. You were not meant to be on the bottom. Everything that you have been through wasn't meant to kill you.

It was to prepare you. You may have been broken, and your spirit may have been shattered. The Potter is waiting to put you back together and place you in the place that He designed specifically for you. You will be restored, my sister. This is not the end of your story. Stay faithful and find out who you are, and then pursue your purpose. Someone is waiting on you.

CHAPTER 8
Living in the Now

I thought that once I had decided to pull my act together and change my way of living, things would be better. How wrong I was. Throughout this book, I have repeated over and over that not everyone would be happy about your transformation. What I found out was most people really didn't care. If you plan on changing thinking that people would cheer you on with a parade or throw a big transformation party, forget about it. That's not going to happen. I also found out what real friendship was all about. Some people stopped talking to me altogether while others slowly drifted away, and then some kept talking to me, but the purpose was to witness my next downfall. Through all of that, I had to understand that people are only in your life for a season. Once you realize that when that season is over, let it go.

When God closes a door, he will open another, and the people you once saw as friends, He will replace them with positive people who really have your best interest at heart. Sounds harsh, but it's true. However, there will be those that have stuck with you through the good and the bad, and they are extremely proud of the changes you have made. It just closes up your circle and rids you of the negativity that once surrounded you. You will learn to appreciate those who supported you during your transition even more. The one thing that I did notice was how I had become the topic of conversation. When I was a mess, I was at the top of the conversation, and after I cleaned up my act, nothing changed. I'll say it again; people will be watching and waiting for you to slip. What you must do is remember to stay focused and remember you are in charge.

You can't let people get into your mind. This will only bring back all the fear and doubt that you fought so hard to get out of your life. I can't say it enough, "Stay Focused." I must admit that I did have some people come to me and earnestly told me they were proud of my transition. What surprised me was that these people were the same ones who doubted me at the beginning of my recovery process. Through this process, I asked God why I had treated myself so badly and allowed myself to go through all this pain? The answer came to me in a dream one night. God let me know that the things that I went through had to happen so that I could understand. I had to find my identity. When I figured out who I was and to whom I belonged, my change came, and now it was time to walk into my true purpose. Other opinions didn't matter. Isn't that powerful? You have got to get it in your heart who you belong to. Stop letting people define your worth. God created you, and He already knows the plans He has for you. Walk-in your purpose and forget about what people say.

They never knew the real you anyway.

That deserves a praise break.

Hallelujah! Know who you are. You were not created to fit in. We have been called out of the darkness and into the light. And light and darkness cannot commune together. Thank you, Lord. I taught preschool children ages 3-5 for several years. The one thing that I have learned about kids is they don't give up easily, but they do get frustrated when they are confronted with a difficult task. Their favorite phrase and we all say it is "I can't do it." As their teacher, it was my responsibility to ensure that anything they set their minds to can do it. We older folks say, "If at first, you don't succeed, try, try again." In the classroom, we said a little chant after group time that says:

I can do it,

I can do it; I can do it.

If I put my heart

And my mind into it,

I can do it.

One day that chant got into my spirit. I told my students to believe they could do whatever they set their minds to, but I wasn't putting that into action in my own life.

Philippians Chapter 4:13 says, "I can do all things through Christ who strengthens me." You can do it. That seems to be the problem. We want victory over our circumstances. We want success, but we don't want to put the work in to achieve our goals. Earlier in the book, I said it's a process one step at a time. You can't skip a step, or you will find yourself right back where you started from. Now, I consult God concerning every area of my life. I pray for direction and clarity for His will in my life. I pray for favor and that he would place people in my life that have achieved where I am trying to get to. Then I l clear my head of clutter and distractions, and I listen. If you don't have a plan in place, I suggest you develop one that includes the direction of how you plan to get where you're trying to go.

If you don't, it's just like baking a cake without a recipe. You're just tossing ingredients into a bowl and hoping for good results. It's the same thing with the goals you have set for your life. If you don't have a plan, you're tossing ideas up in the air with no direction or plan to follow. Through this process, I have learned that your career and your purpose are two different goals. I used to think by working in the children's church; I was walking in my purpose since I taught preschool and have worked in the school system. I found out just because I teach for a living doesn't mean it's my purpose. It became overwhelming after a while, and I felt bad. I realized that I wasn't effective as I should have been in trying to do both. Teaching is my passion, but it is not the purpose that God has designed for me in helping to build His Kingdom. Make sure you check yourself on that. The Bible says, "Seek ye first the kingdom of God and everything else will be added." Seek God first, and He will reveal your purpose to you.

Friends, I have learned so much during this journey, and I'm still learning every day. The most important thing that I have learned is the importance of an effective prayer life.

I remember when I was at my lowest.

The thing that brought me through was prayer. I didn't always have that. I was so angry at one point that I thought God had forgotten me, and I did not need to pray. It didn't take long to realize how wrong I was about that.

Those were the most heartbreaking moments in my life. You must stay connected to the source. James 5:16 says that "The effectual fervent prayer of a righteous man availeth much." Prayer is your connection to the source. Some may say God already knows my needs, and that may be true.

It is also true that he wants to hear it from you. Not only does He want to bless you with your needs, but He also wants to bless you with the desires of your heart. In Third John 2, it says, "Beloved I wish that thou mayest prosper and be in health even as you soul all prospers. "Glory to

God." Isn't He an awesome God? You may be saying, "I don't know how to pray or what to pray." I know you hear people who pray so elegantly, and others seem to pray until the glory comes down. You are God's friend, and He knows your name. When I talk to God, I talk as though He is right there with me, and really, He is. I start by praising Him for all that He is and for all He has already done and for what He will do. I then repent with my whole heart. That means when I ask for forgiveness, it is with the intent not to repeat the same sin over again. I know you're thinking, really. Yes, really.

Remember, we can have what we say.

Ask God to search your heart and if it's anything that goes against His will for your life and the upbuilding of the Kingdom, ask him to remove it. I dare you to try Him. After repenting, just talk to Him. He is your Father. I tell Him what's on my mind, the things that I am angry or sorrowful for, my hurts, and my disappointments. I also tell Him my desires, along with my wants and my needs. Then, I put praise on it. Hallelujah, don't we serve a good, good God? Let's stop here and offer up a prayer to the "Most High."

Father God,

We come in the name of Your son Jesus Christ. Lord, we want to take the time to say thank you. Lord, we want to thank you for all that you have done for us. And all that you are going to do in our lives. Lord, if you don't do anything else for us, we still say thank you. Lord, we come humbly before the throne, asking your forgiveness for the things that we have done willingly and for the things that we have done, not thinking that it was sinful, but it was not pleasing in your sight. We repent with our whole heart. Lord, we love you in spirit and in truth.

In Jesus Name, Amen

Isn't it sweet to know that we serve a God that forgives us and does not keep a record of what we have done once we repent? I know that I am grateful. I know you're probably thinking all that is good, but what's next?

How do I move into this new life?

It all comes back to faith and what you believe. It starts with the plan that we have been talking about. Earlier in the book, we talked about the vision board.

I still have my very first vision board.

As I accomplish things that I put on my board, I check it off my list, and I'm constantly adding to my vision.

God wants us to live a good life on this side as well. Don't put God in a box and underestimate what He can and will do in your life. Paul said, "Write the vision and make it plain."

I remember when I didn't have a vision.

Now, I celebrate any accomplishments that I have achieved, no matter how small. I want you to understand that you were uniquely made with a purpose in mind that only you can fulfill. Stop doubting and put fear in its place. Trust God and step into your destiny Somebody needs you.

God never ceases to amaze me as He continues to move in my life.

Like many of you, I still have those days when I don't see any changes in my situation, or I can't see where I am making a difference. During those moments, He reminds me that I have a purpose to fulfill, which is to tell how He brought me through it all and not me on my own My purpose is to share my story. My first step was writing this book and sharing my journey with you. This is my testimony of how God took someone broken, crushed, and who had given up on life and turned her around through some painful but needed experiences. God took this shattered vessel and molded me back together into a vessel to be used to draw others into the Kingdom. If you've never experienced anything, how can you tell someone else how to overcome it? If you have never been homeless, abandoned, abused, depressed, addicted to drugs or alcohol, you can't effectively minister to this group of souls that feel lost in this world. You have a story to tell, and now is the time to tell it. As I said earlier, it's all up to you. No one can tell your story but you.

Step out on faith. The time has come to bring healing to not only yourself but to others as well. Trust God as you seek Him. Ask Him to reveal to you What's His will for your life. Meditate on the scriptures. Since I have been studying the bible instead of just reading it, God has revealed so much to me. I can see into the scriptures as though I were there. And feel how those living during that time must have been like. I ask God daily to give me the wisdom to understand as I read. Things I don't understand I ask questions, write down my questions, and do the research. God is not going to send you out there, unequipped. God asks you to do anything that He has already paved the way for you to do it.

It all goes back to trusting God and having faith that He will never leave you or forsake you. I choose to stand on God's word, and you should too. Won't you trust Him and let Him show you that He is not a man that He should lie? Every promise that he made, He will fulfill. Yesterday is gone, and tomorrow may never come, but you have today. Start your new beginning today. Don't wait until the battle is over. Praise Him for the victory right now. I love you with the love of Christ and thank you for taking this journey with me.

Will you "Let go and let God?"

Please take this moment and pray with me:

Father God,

I thank you in the Name of Jesus for allowing me to share my story.

I thank you, Father, that when others didn't believe that You could use someone as broken and confused as me, You believed and appointed me to be a blessing to others. I thank you, Lord, that when I felt unworthy to answer the call, You placed the right people in my life to encourage me and let me know that this was my time. I thank you, Lord, for, in the still of the night, You speak to me with a gentle voice.

I thank you for Your presence.

Lord, may this book be a blessing to the Kingdom. I praise You, and I honor You

In Jesus Name, Amen.

FINAL THOUGHTS...
It's All Up to You

Everything that you ever hope to achieve in your life you are already equipped to do. From the very beginning, before you were a thought in the minds of your parents, there was a purpose-designed by God specifically for you. There is no dream that is too big that you cannot reach. There are no goals that you have set for yourself that you can't achieve if you just believe and reach out to catch your dreams in your mind. We were not all fortunate to come from wealthy, loving backgrounds. Not everyone had the option to attend an Ivy League school. When all that is said, we still have the potential to move far beyond where we are now. Life is choice-driven, and the choices that we make today are the only choices that matter. Yesterday is gone, and for some of us, good ridden. The day for what used to be has set with the sun. And the window to what can be is opening with each new dawn. The time has come to stop letting your past control your future.

You are worth more than your mind can conceive. The bad breaks that life seemed to deal with; you were not meant to beat you down or keep you down. Although going through, it didn't feel as though any good could ever come from the bruises and pain you endured.

Little could I have known that all these battle scars were purposed to prepare me to be what He designed me to be with a purpose in mind that only I could fulfill. Some of us would say that I never had a dream. I never saw a need to dream, or maybe I once had a dream, but that's all it was. A dream can never come fulfilled if all it was only an idea and not put into action. No matter what we say, we all had a dream where we saw ourselves as kids, where we would love to go, and what we would like to be when we grew up.

As adults, we have dreams of our future mates, what our children will be like, places we would like to visit, and where we would like to live our perfect lives working in our perfect careers.

What happened to those dreams?

Life. It's just that clear-cut and simple. Today is a new day. It's time to put all those bad breaks behind you. Destiny awaits you, and it has your name on it. Put a praise on it! I encourage you to stop looking behind. What was, was. What can be is all up to you. No more shackles are holding you back. It's time to break free from the bondage of the past and move forward into the life that you were created to live. It's time to put your faith to work. Assign your faith a destination. No more what I could have or should have done. It's time just to do it. Faith without works is dead. Wake up your dreams and find your hope. Become a prisoner of hope and cling to it. Become a destiny seeker. There are no more tomorrows. Today is the beginning of your future. Nothing is impossible if you just believe. Dare to dream and dare to believe woman of God. Today is a new day. New day, New way!! Remember, at the end of the day, "It's All Up to You."

ABOUT THE AUTHOR

Denise Gardner lives in rural North Carolina. She is the mother of one daughter, DeAja, who is the light of her life. She is active in Evangelism at her church and has a future goal of starting a Women's Ministry in her community.

CPSIA information can be obtained
at www.ICGtesting.com
Printed in the USA
FSHW021635290321
79885FS